Golf

First published in Great Britain in 1996 by Brockhampton Press,
a member of the Hodder Headline Group, 20 Bloomsbury Street, London WC1B 3QA

This series of little gift books was made by Frances Banfield, Kate Brown, Laurel Clark,
Penny Clarke, Clive Collins, Melanie Cumming, Nick Diggory, Deborah Gill, David Goodman,
Douglas Hall, Maureen Hill, Nick Hutchison, John Hybert, Kate Hybert, Douglas Ingram,
Simon London, Patrick McCreeth, Morse Modaberi, Tara Neill, Anne Newman, Grant Oliver,
Michelle Rogers, Nigel Soper, Karen Sullivan and Nick Wells.

ISBN 1 86019 471 0
A copy of the CIP data is available from the British Library upon request.

Produced for Brockhampton Press by The Flame Tree Publishing,
part of The Foundry Creative Media Company Limited,
The Long House, Antrobus Road, London W4 5HY

Printed and bound in Italy by L.E.G.O. Spa.

CELEBRATION

Golf

Selected by Karen Sullivan

After an abominable round of golf, a man is
known to have slit his wrists with a razor
blade, and, having bandaged them, to have
stumbled into the locker room and enquired of
his partner, 'What time tomorrow?'

Alistair Cooke

All holes are blind to those who cannot play.

Gerald Batchelor

I get upset over a bad shot just like anyone else. But it's silly to let the game get to you. When I miss a shot I just think what a beautiful day it is. And what pure fresh air I'm breathing. Then I take a deep breath. I have to do that. That's what gives me the strength to break the club.

Bob Hope

I guess there is nothing that will get your mind off everything like golf will. I have never been depressed enough to take up the game, but they say you can get so sore at yourself that you forget to hate your enemies.

Will Rogers

GOLFING
IN SOUTHERN ENGLAND AND ON THE CONTINENT
PUBLISHED BY THE SOUTHERN RAILWAY

There are certain things you don't believe in. The Easter Bunny.
Campaign promises. The Abominable Snowman. A husband with
lipstick on his collar. And a guy who tells you he shot a 59 on his own
ball. Out of town, of course.

Jim Murray

What other people may find in poetry or art museums, I find in the
flight of a good drive – the white ball sailing up into the blue sky,
growing smaller and smaller, then suddenly reaching its apex, curving,
falling and finally dropping to the turf to roll some more, just the way
I planned it.

Arnold Palmer

60e Année. N° 38 — Le Numéro : 1 fr. 50 — Samedi 23 Septembre 1922

LA VIE PARISIENNE

HEROUARD

Rédaction, Administration et Publicité : 29, rue Tronchet, Paris.

Golf is a game in which the ball lies poorly and the players well.

Art Rosenbaum

If there is any larceny in a man, golf will bring it out.

Paul Gallico

I was three over: one over a house, one over a patio, and one over a swimming pool.

George Brett

When you play the game for fun, it's fun. When you play it for a living, it's a game of sorrows.

Gary Player

One minute it's fear and loathing, but hit a couple of good shots, and you're on top of the world.

Jack Nicholson

Fore!
Gleneagles
The Golf Course the Great
in
Scotland
The Caledonian Railway

ST. ANDREWS

GUIDE FREE FROM TOWN CLERK, ST. ANDREWS, FIFE

Train services and fares from  **BRITISH RAILWAYS** stations, offices and agencies

A game of golf is usually played between two, sometimes four friends. Each player tries to urge his golf ball into a special hole in the grass by tapping it with one of his bundle of sticks. When the ball eventually drops into the hole the golfer remembers the number of whacks it took him and, if his friend is watching, writes that number down on his scorecard. After doing this 18 times the friends add up their scores to find the winner. As in receiving a prison sentence, or the news of a multiple birth of offspring, a low number is hoped for. After working out who is the winner, the losers all say 'Well done!' and silently accompany their ex-friend back to the club house.

Frank Muir, *One Over Par*

The only way of really finding out a man's true character is to play golf with him. In no other walk of life does the cloven hoof so quickly display itself.

P.G. Wodehouse

One thing that's always available on a golf course is advice. If you play like I do, you think everybody knows something you don't know. If I see a bird fly over, I think he's going to tell me something.

Buddy Hackett

I'd like to thank the press from the bottom of my ... well, from the heart of my bottom, anyway.

Nick Faldo

I don't like watching golf on TV. I can't stand whispering.

David Brenner

Man blames fate for other accidents but feels personally responsible for a hole in one.

Martha Beckman

During the Second World War, Lester Pearson (then in the Canadian High Commission) went to play golf at Roehampton in London. Just as he was about to drive off, his caddy advised him 'to slice well over to the right, farther over than usual, sir, because there is a time bomb on the left there by the red flat on the 18th fairway.' As if golf isn't a difficult enough game!

Mad Mac, for many years Max Faulkner's caddie, had another client who looked after him very well. A quiet man, a bit of a recluse, he liked his round of golf, but preferred to play with imaginary clubs – which Mad Mac of course carried for him.

The fellow would go through the motions, with Mac supplying the sound effects, the swishing of the club, the crack as it hit the ball. Then Mac would cry: 'Oh, lovely shot, sir. Two hundred and twenty yards, just down the middle of the fairway.'

Then Mac hoisted the imaginary bag on to his shoulder and they'd walk down the fairway. Mac handed his client a 7-iron, and watched him make his stroke.

'Whaaacckkk. Oh, well done, sir.'

One day they were going round, and had got to the 11th when the people behind them caught up. They were fascinated by what they'd been seeing. One of them asked Mac what on earth was going on, imaginary clubs, swiping at thin air and so on.

'Ssshh,' said Mac, a finger to his lips. 'Don't you disturb him. He's four under par and that the best he's ever done on this course.'

'What do you mean?' cried the fellow. 'It's crazy. You've got no clubs, no ball, what's it all for?'

'I'm not sure myself,' said Mac. 'Not a word to him, though. He hasn't got a car either, but he gives me a tenner a week to keep it clean.'

Peter Allis, *Bedside Golf*

 17

I'd like to see the fairways more narrow. Then everyone would have to play from the rough, not just me.

Seve Ballesteros

There are three ways of learning golf: by study, which is the most wearisome, by imitation which is the most fallacious, and by experience, which is the most bitter.

Robert Browning

No one who ever had lessons would have a swing like mine.

Lee Trevino

NORTH BERWICK

Illustrated Booklet free from Town Clerk or any L·N·E·R Agency

IT'S
QUICKER
BY RAIL

At Jinja there is both a hotel and golf course. The latter is, I believe, the only course in the world which posts a special rule that the player may remove his ball from hippopotamus footprints.

Evelyn Waugh

If God wants to produce the ideal golfer then He should create a being with a set of unequal arms and likewise legs, an elbow-free left arm, knees which hinge sideways and a ribless torso from which emerges, at an angle of 45 degrees, a stretched neck fitted with one colour-blind eye stuck firmly on the left side. And please God, let him be British.

Chris Plumridge, *Almost Straight Down the Middle*

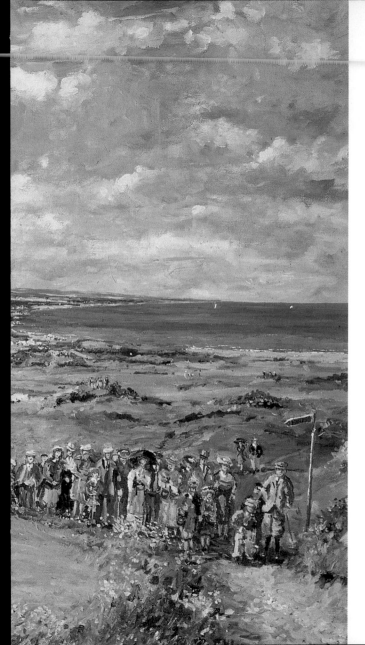

Golf is not a game, it's bondage. It was obviously devised by a man torn with guilt, eager to atone for his sins.

Jim Murray

Every time you hit a golf shot, there are people who like it and there are people who dislike it. If it goes in the hole, the people who are pulling for you are patting you on the back. And the guy who is pulling for Niklaus says, That lucky SOB – he made a hole in one.

Lee Trevino

I know I'm getting better at golf because I'm hitting fewer spectators.

Gerald R. Ford

CRUDEN BAY

TRAVEL BY L·N·E·R

"E HOLIDAY HANDBOOK" 1140 PAGES ILLUSTRATIONS IN PHOTOGRAVURE DETAILS OF ACCOMMODATIO
MAPS AND STREET PLANS FROM BOOKSELLERS AND L·N·E·R AGENCIES PRICE 6D.

In the Bob Hope Golf Classic the participation of President Gerald Ford was more than enough to remind you that the nuclear button was at one stage at the disposal of a man who might have either pressed it by mistake or else pressed it deliberately in order to obtain room service.

Clive James

I'd rather have him as a partner than an opponent ... That's because he can be pretty sneaky. He'll get out there on the first tee and try to make a match. The first thing he does is talk his opponents out of their handicaps.

Bing Crosby about Bob Hope, *Bob Hope, Thanks for the Memory*

BOVRIL

FOR HEALTH STRENGTH AND BEAUTY

For me, it's a game to be
played with fresh air in
your lungs and joy in
your heart.

Peter Alliss, *More Bedside Golf*

The golfer was transported to Heaven and found it was a magnificent golf course flanked by trees, like a celestial Pinehurst. With his angel guide he set out to explore and the first player he saw was shaking to cut the corner of a dog leg, a feat demanding carry of at least three hundred yards.

'That shot will be a miracle,' observed the newcomer, 'who does he think he is – St Peter?'

'It happens to be St Peter,' whispered the angel, 'but he thinks he's Arnold Palmer.'

Tom Scott and Geoffrey Cousins, *The Wit of Golf*

If you go out with a man who plays golf, your biggest problem will be not to laugh the first time you see him in action. Once they get on the course, the most sober, steadfast and demure individuals suddenly blossom out like court jesters, in the most brilliant colours and fashions – lemon-yellow caps, pale blue anoraks, cherry-pink trousers. And when they wiggle their feet to get their stance right they look exactly like cats preparing to pee.

Jilly Cooper, *Men and Super Men*

I played golf with a priest the other day ... He shot par-par-par-par-par. Finally, I said to him, 'Father, if you're playing golf like this, you haven't been saving many souls lately.'

Sam Snead

He has won about as much money playing golf as I've paid on lessons.

Bob Hope on Arnold Palmer

Arnold has more people watching him park the car than we do out on the course.

Lee Trevino

- THE GOLFERS OF St ANDREW -

The pat on the back, the arm around the shoulder, the prize for what was done right, and the sympathetic nod for what wasn't are as much a part of life as golf itself.

Gerald Ford

Sometimes it's difficult for spectators to know where to stand at all, with any guarantee of safety.

Peter Alliss, *More Bedside Golf*

Politics, like music and golf, is best learned at an early age.

Lawrence Welk

Playing golf with any President is handy. If you hit a ball in the rough and it stops near a tree, the tree becomes a Secret Service man and moves away.

Bob Hope, *Bob Hope, Thanks for the Memory*

Golf is so popular simply because it is the best game in the world at which to be bad.

A. A. Milne, *Not that it Matters*

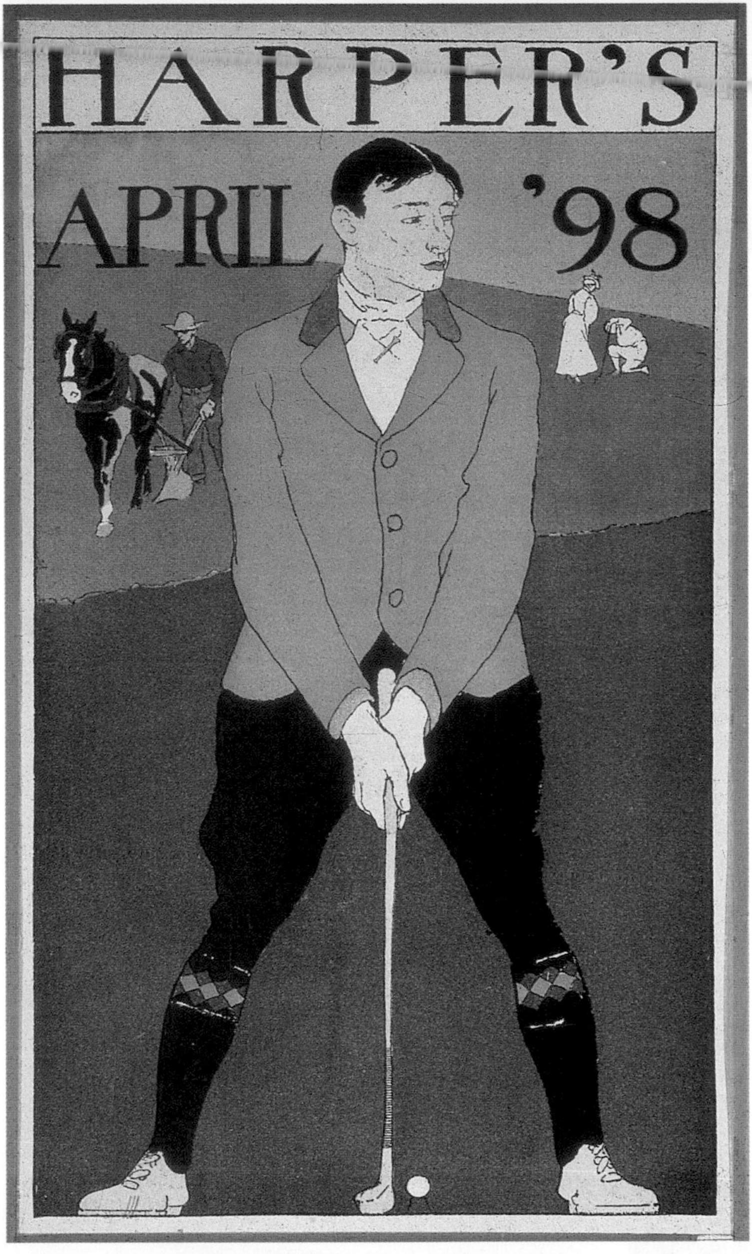
HARPER'S
APRIL '98

THE GOLFING GIRL

A TRUE LINE DRIVE

THE GOLFING GIRL AND ALL HER
FRIENDS PLAY GOOD GOLF ON
ALL THE GOLF COURSES OF THE
DELIGHTFUL DISTRICTS SERVED BY

THE CALEDONIAN
RAILWAY.

DONALD A. MATHESON, GENERAL MANAGER

Short putts are missed because it is not physically possible to make the little ball travel over uncertain ground for three or four feet with any degree of regularity.

Walter Hagen

Putting is like wisdom – partly a natural gift and partly the accumulation of experience.

Arnold Palmer

I never pray to God to make a putt. I pray to God to help me react good if I miss a putt.

Chi Chi Rodriguez

President Ford was playing golf with ice hockey star Gordie Howe. At the 12th hole, Howe conceded a two-foot putt to his distinguished opponent. Ford insisted on taking the shot and missed. 'We won't count that one,' said Howe. Pointing to the reporters and Secret Service men at the edge of the green, Ford said, 'Maybe you won't, but they will.'

Fitness counts for less in golf than in any other game, luck enters into every minute of the contest, and all play is purely incidental to, and conditioned by, gamesmanship.

Stephen Potter, *The Complete Upmanship*

If it wasn't for golf, I'd be a caddie today.

George Archer

There are two things not long for this world – dogs that chase cars and pro golfers who chip for pars.

Lee Trevino

The City Golf Club in London is unique among such organizations in not possessing a golf course, ball, tee, caddy or bag. Its whole premises just off Fleet Street do not contain a single photograph of anything that approaches a golfing topic ...

Stephen Pile, *The Least Successful Golf Club*

Particularly pleasing is the story of Queen Alexandra muddling golf with croquet and, when on the green, gaily hitting her husband's golf-ball away from the hole and then pushing her own in.

Arthur Marshall, *Sunny Side Up*

The ball's got to stop somewhere. It might as well be at the bottom of the hole.

Lee Trevino

All I've got against golf is that it takes you so far from the club house.

Eric Linklater, *Poet's Pub*

Playing the game I have learned the meaning of humility. It has given me an understanding of the futility of human effort.

Abba Eban

Golf is a terrible, hopeless addiction, it seems: it makes its devotees willing to trudge miles in any manner of weather, lugging a huge, incommodious and appallingly heavy bag with them, in pursuit of a tiny and fantastically expensive ball, in a fanatical attempt to direct it into a hole the size of a beer glass half a mile away. If anything could be better calculated to convince one of the essential lunacy of the human race, I haven't found it. And yet it gives one a breath of hope when one perceives that it's most ardent devotees are, somewhere very deep inside, fully aware of the absurdity of their consuming passion.

Mike Seabrook, *One Over Par*

Years ago we discovered the exact point, the dead centre of middle age. It occurs when you are too young to take up golf and too old to rush up to the net.

Franklin P. Adams, *Nods and Becks*

NORTH BERWICK

ILLUSTRATED BOOKLET FREE FROM TOWN CLERK OR ANY L·N·E·R AGENCY

Golf is a game the aim of which is to hit a small ball into an even smaller hole with weapons singularly ill-designed for the purpose.

Sir Winston Churchill

If you are caught on a golf course during a storm and are afraid of lightning, hold up a 1-iron. Not even God can hit a 1-iron.

Lee Trevino

Golf is the most fun you can have without taking your clothes off.

Chi Chi Rodriguez

You can always tell a golfer. Part 1.

BY HIS CONSTANTLY REMOVING
IMAGINARY WORMCASTS

You can always tell a golfer. Part 2.

BY HIS CURIOUS STANCE WHEN WAITING FOR THE TRAIN

Nobody ever swung the golf club too slowly.

Bobby Jones

Keeping the head still is golf's one universal unarguable fundamental.

Jack Nicklaus

Never give a golfer an ultimatum unless you're prepared to lose.

Abigail Van Buren

One day I played nine holes with Jack Nicklaus and I beat him on two of the holes. I knew I was a good player, but that's when I knew I was a great player.

Chi Chi Rodriguez

He enjoys that perfect peace, that peace beyond all understanding, which comes at its maximum only to the man who has given up golf.

P.G. Wodehouse

Golf: A game in which one endeavours to control a ball with implements ill adapted for the purpose.

Woodrow Wilson

Very proud of having walked around with him for the first time, Daddy's Little Angel couldn't wait to tell everyone about it. 'My father is the best golfer in the whole world,' she claimed. 'He can play for hours and hours and hours and hardly ever lets the ball go into those little holes.'

From *Great Golf Jokes*

Golf, like measles, should be caught young, for, if postponed to riper years, the results may be serious.

P.G. Wodehouse, *A Mixed Threesome*

To that man, age brought only golf instead of wisdom.

George Bernard Shaw

You can always tell a golfer. Part 3.

BY HIS UNFAILING INSTINCT
TO KEEP HIS EYE
ON A BALL

When miracles happen on the golf course, it is
important to know how to respond to them.
Songwriter Hoagy Carmichael, an avid golfer, once
teed up on a par-three hole, picked up a club and hit
the ball. It bounced once on the green, hit the pin
and dropped in for a hole in one. Hoagy didn't say a
word, but took another ball from his pocket, teed up,
then observed, 'I think I've got the idea now.'

Buddy Hackett, *The Truth About Golf and Other Lies*

You can always
tell a golfer.
Part 5.

BY HIS STRANGE
CALLS WHEN CON-
FRONTED WITH AN
OBSTACLE IN HIS
MORNING'S PROGRESS
TO THE STATION

If I died ... it meant I couldn't play golf. No way was I giving up golf, so I gave up drinking.

Bob Hope

I'm the best. I just haven't played yet.

Muhammad Ali, on golf

I owe everything to golf. Where else could a guy with an IQ like mine make this much money?

Hubert Green

Some of us worship in churches, some in synagogues, some on golf courses.

Adlai Stevenson

By the time you can afford to lose a ball, you can't hit it that far.

Anonymous

Golfaholics are never content when the round is over. They want 'just one more' hole to take away the bad taste of the previous 18. Or they insist on working out their miseries on the putting green hour after hour, oblivious to other plans for the afternoon – like a wedding. Theirs.

Mark Oman, *Portrait of a Golfaholic*

I just hope I don't have to explain all the times I've used His name in vain when I get up there.

Bob Hope

There are two things you can do with your head down – play golf and pray.

Lee Trevino

You know you're having a bad day when ...

You run over your own foot with your electric cart.

Other golfers have nicknamed you 'Shank'

Your shoes are filled with enough sand to open your own private beach club.

You've lifted your head so often you have a crick in your neck.

The rest of your foursome huddles behind a bench as you tee off.

Your tee-off time for tomorrow has been revoked.

Your club membership has been revoked.

Your woods are too embarrassed to come out of the bag.

The course pro introduces you to a tennis instructor.

The course superintendent threatens you with legal action.

Birds flying south readjust their flight pattern to let you hit.

People are offering you good prices for your clubs.

Between the 9th and 10th holes, life insurance salesmen approach you in the clubhouse.

Richard Mintzer, *The Unofficial Golfer's Handbook*

There are two kinds of golf –
golf and tournament golf.

Bobby Jones

Golf: A day spent in a round of
strenuous idleness.

William Wordsworth

My swing is so bad I look like a caveman killing his lunch.

Lee Trevino

Like life, golf can be humbling. However, little good comes from brooding about mistakes we've made. The next shot, in golf or in life, is the big one.

Grantland Rice

Every competitor who is awake soon enough sees the necessity for preparing a speech against the contingency of the medal being presented to him in the evening. Nor is anyone much crushed when all is over, and he has not won. If he does well, it was but that putt, that bad lie, that bunker. If his score is bad, what of it? Even the best are off their game occasionally. Next time it will be different.

Sir Walter Simpson

The least thing upset him on the links. He missed short putts because of the uproar of butterflies in the adjoining meadows.

P.G. Wodehouse

It's a marriage. If I had to choose between my wife and my putter – I'd miss her.

Gary Player

I'm a golfaholic, no question about that. Counselling wouldn't help me. They'd have to put me in prison, and then I'd talk the warden into building a hole or two and teach him how to play.

Lee Trevino

Some players today play two or three tournaments, get tired, and then take a couple of weeks off. I couldn't wait to get to the next tournament. If they're tired they should go to bed early.

Ben Hogan

Once in Scotland I played with the most fanatical golfer I've ever met. We were just teeing off on the 15th where the green lies next to the main road. He was in the middle of his backswing when a row of funeral cars came past. He stopped, took off his cap, held it over his heart and bowed his head. I was impressed. I said 'You're a man who shows real respect for the deceased.' He said, 'It's only fair. She was a good wife to me for 37 years.'

Bob Monkhouse

My car absolutely will not run unless my golf clubs are in the trunk.

Bruce Berlet

CRUDEN BAY

BY EAST COAST ROUTE

ILLUSTRATED BOOKLET FREE FROM PASSENGER MANAGERS,
LIVERPOOL STREET STATION, LONDON, E.C.2; L·N·E·R YORK; OR ANY L·N·E·R ENQUIRY OFFICE.

The difference between a sand bunker and water is the difference between a car crash and an airplane crash. You have a chance of recovering from a car crash.

Bobby Jones

The longer you play, the better chance the better player has of winning.

Jack Nicklaus

Golf is not relaxation, golf is everything, golf is a philosophy, it's a religion, absolutely, I mean really absolutely.

Sir Bob Reid

For the golfer, Nature loses her significance. Larks, the casts of worms, the buzzing of bees, and even children are hateful to him ... Winds cease to be east, south, west or north. They are ahead, behind or sideways, and the sky is bright or dark, according to the state of the game.

Sir W.G. Simpson, *The Art of Golf*

My gaaad! I've got socks older than you.

Lee Trevino to a 27-year-old opponent

Golf is a good walk spoiled.

Mark Twain

It's not whether you win or lose – but whether I win or lose.

Sandy Lyle

Golf's predictable structure is both comforting and relaxing. We can almost predict the exact words our playing partners will use to set up the game on the first tee. This predictability provides a safe harbour for a few hours to avoid some of the storms of the everyday world. Golf absorbs our minds, and the mental tribulations of our lives are put on hold as we wrestle with errant drives, pulled approach shots and missed putts.

Dr Richard H. Coop

THE GOLFING GIRL

"WELL OUT"
ON
THE TRUE LINE

THE GOLFING GIRL AND ALL HER FRIENDS PLAY GOOD GOLF ON ALL THE GOLF COURSES
OF THE DELIGHTFUL DISTRICTS SERVED BY

THE CALEDONIAN RAILWAY

SUCH AS					
ABERDEEN	BLAIRGOWRIE	DAVIDSON'S MAINS	JUNIPER GREEN	MOFFAT	ST FILLANS
ABINGTON	BRIDGE OF ALLAN	DUNBLANE	KINGSKNOWE	MONIFIETH	SALTCOATS
ALYTH	CALLANDER	DUNOON	KIRRIEMUIR	MONTROSE	STIRLING
ARBROATH	CARLUKE	EAST KILBRIDE	LANARK	OBAN	STONEHAVEN
AUCHTERARDER	CARNOUSTIE	EDZELL	LAURENCEKIRK	PEEBLES	STRATHAVEN
BARNTON	COMRIE	FORFAR	LOCH AWE	PERTH	UPLAWMOOR
BIGGAR	CRAWFORD	GOUROCK	MACHRIHANISH	ROBERTON	WEMYSS BAY
BISHOPTON	CRIEFF	IRVINE	MILLPORT	ROTHESAY	WHITECRAIGS

BY ROWLAND HILDER

Come to Britain
for GOLF

Published by the Travel Association of Great Britain and Northern Ireland (Export Division of the British Travel and Holidays Board) and printed in Great Britain by W. S. Cowell Ltd, London & Ipswich.

It doesn't matter how many Open championships or titles you may have won. When you stand on the tee at a Ryder Cup match and play for your country, your stomach rumbles like a kid turning up for his first tournament.

Arnold Palmer

Give me golf clubs, fresh air and a beautiful partner, and you can keep my golf clubs and the fresh air.

Jack Benny

He took a swing like a man with a wasp under his shirt and his pants on fire, trying to impale a butterfly on the end of a scythe.

Paul Gallico, *Golf is a Nice Friendly Game*

An *alter kocker* is a man who can no longer do something that he once could ... There are certain activities that are recognizable for old people that only an *alter kocker* gets involved in and golf is one.

Jackie Mason, *How to Talk Jewish*

Dan would rather play golf than have sex anyday.

Marilyn Quayle

I did not want to turn to playing golf, because golf is about as much exercise as shuffling cards.

Bill Cosby, *Time Flies*

Notes on Illustrations

Page viii *Harry Vardon, John Henry Taylor and James Braid, the "Great Triumvirate", June 21st*, by Clement Flower (*Illustrated London News*). Courtesy of The Bridgeman Art Library; **Page 3** *Golfing – In Southern England and the Continent,* Advertisement published, by the Southern Railway (Private Collection). Courtesy of The Bridgeman Art Library; **Page 5** *Cover of La Vie Parisienne, 1922* (Private Collection). Courtesy of The Bridgeman Art Library; **Page 6-7** *View of Military Players at St Andrews*, by English School (Royal & Ancient Golf Club, St Andrew's). Courtesy of The Bridgeman Art Library; **Page 9** *Fore! Gleneagle.* Courtesy of Hobbs Golf Collection, Northumberland; **Page 10** *St Andrews, Guide Free from Town Clerk.* Courtesy of Hobbs Golf Collection, Northumberland; **Page 13** *Golfers on the Old Course, St Andrews.* Courtesy of Hobbs Golf Collection, Northumberland; **Page 15** *Teeing Off*, by Lawrence Toynbee (The Fine Art Society, London). Courtesy of The Bridgeman Art Library; **Page 19** *North Berwick, Illustrated Booklet Free from the Town Clerk.* Courtesy of Hobbs Golf Collection, Northumberland; **Page 20-1** *Westward Ho!* Courtesy of Hobbs Golf Collection; **Page 23** *Portrait of John Whyte Melville of Bennochy and Strathkinness, Captain of the Club, 1823*, by Sir Francis Grant (Royal & Ancient Golf Club, St Andrew's). Courtesy of The Bridgeman Art Library; **Page 24-5** *The Fifth Tee, St Andrew's, 1921*, by John Sutton (Eaton Gallery, Princes Arcade, London). Courtesy of The Bridgeman Art Library; **Page 27** *Cruden Bay Travel, by LNER.* Courtesy of Hobbs Golf Collection, Northumberland; **Page 29** *Bovril, Health, Strength & Beauty.* Courtesy of Hobbs Golf Collection, Northumberland; **Page 30-1** *Prestwick.* Courtesy of Hobbs Golf Collection, Northumberland; **Page 35** *Edinburgh from the Bruntisfield Golf Links*, by Francis Nicholson (Victoria & Albert Museum, London). Courtesy of The Bridgeman Art Library; **Page 36** *Golfers at St Andrews*, by Jean Carrau (Private Collection). Courtesy of The Bridgeman Art Library; **Page 39** Cover of *Harper's Magazine,* April 1898. (Lords Gallery, London). Courtesy of The Bridgeman Art Library; **Page 40** *The Golfing Girl Caledonian Railway.* Courtesy of Hobbs Golf Collection, Northumberland; **Page 42-3** *John Ball about to Play at Hoylake 1895.* Courtesy of Hobbs Golf Collection, Northumberland; **Page 45** *Child Playing Golf*, by Aelbert Cuyp (Private Collection). Courtesy of The Bridgeman Art Library; **Page 47** *USA: Early this Century.* Courtesy of Hobbs Golf Collection, Northumberland; **Page 51** *North Berwick – It's Quicker, by Rail.* Courtesy of Hobbs Golf Collection, Northumberland; **Page 53** *"How Can You Detect Your True Golfer from the Ordinary Man in the Street"*, by William Heath Robinson (Chris Beetles Ltd, London). Courtesy of The Bridgeman Art Library; **Page 54** *"How Can You Detect Your True Golfer from the Ordinary Man in the Street"*, by William Heath Robinson

(Chris Beetles Ltd, London). Courtesy of The Bridgeman Art Library; **Page 57**"*How Can You Detect Your True Golfer from the Ordinary Man in the Street*", by William Heath Robinson (Chris Beetles Ltd, London). Courtesy of The Bridgeman Art Library; **Page 59** "*How Can You Detect Your True Golfer from the Ordinary Man in the Street*", by William Heath Robinson (Chris Beetles Ltd, London). Courtesy of The Bridgeman Art Library; **Page 60** "*How Can You Detect Your True Golfer from the Ordinary Man in the Street*", by William Heath Robinson (Chris Beetles Ltd, London). Courtesy of The Bridgeman Art Library; **Page 62** *Old & Young*, by Tom Morris. Courtesy Hobbs Golf Collection, Northumberland; **Page 66-7** *The First Tee at Royal St George's, Sandwich*, by Herbert John Finn (Gavin Graham Gallery, London). Courtesy of The Bridgeman Art Library; **Page 69** *Gentleman Playing Golf, Calendar Illustration for October* (Stapleton Collection). Courtesy of The Bridgeman Art Library; **Page 70** *The East Coast – Ideal for Golfing:* Poster for the Great Eastern Railway, by Hassall (Private Collection). Courtesy of The Bridgeman Art Library; **Page 72-3** *Michael Brown Painting*. Courtesy of Hobbs Golf Collection, Northumberland; **Page 75** *Cruden Bay, by East Coast Route*. Courtesy of Hobbs Golf Collection, Northumberland; **Page 79** *The Golfing Girl: The Caledonian Railway*. Courtesy of Hobbs Golf Collection, Northumberland; **Page 80** *Come to Britain for Golf*. Courtesy of Hobbs Golf Collection, Northumberland; **Page 83** *Bunkered Golfer*. Courtesy of Hobbs Golf Collection, Northumberland.

Acknowledgements: The Publishers wish to thank everyone who gave permission to reproduce the quotes in this book. Every effort has been made to contact the copyright holders, but in the event that an oversight has occurred, the publishers would be delighted to rectify any omissions in future editions of this book. Children's quotes printed courtesy of Herne Hill School; *Bedside Golf* and *More Bedside Golf*, Peter Alliss, reprinted courtesy of HarperCollins; *The Unofficial Golfer's Handbook*, Richard Mintzer, reprinted courtesy of Plume Books, a division of Penguin Books; *Portrait of a Golfaholic*, Mark Oman, reprinted courtesy of Contemporary Books; *Almost Straight Down the Middle*, Chris Plumridge, reprinted courtesy of Queen Anne Press; *One Over Par*, Mike Seabrook and Peter Alliss, reprinted courtesy of H.F. and G. Witherby Ltd, a division of Cassell; jokes by Glenn Liebman appear in *Golf Shorts*, published by Robson Books; *The Wit of Golf*, Tom Scott and Geoffrey Cousins, reprinted courtesy of Leslie Frewan Publishers; *Golf Talk*, compiled by Laurence Bilenson, Peter Pauper Press, Inc.